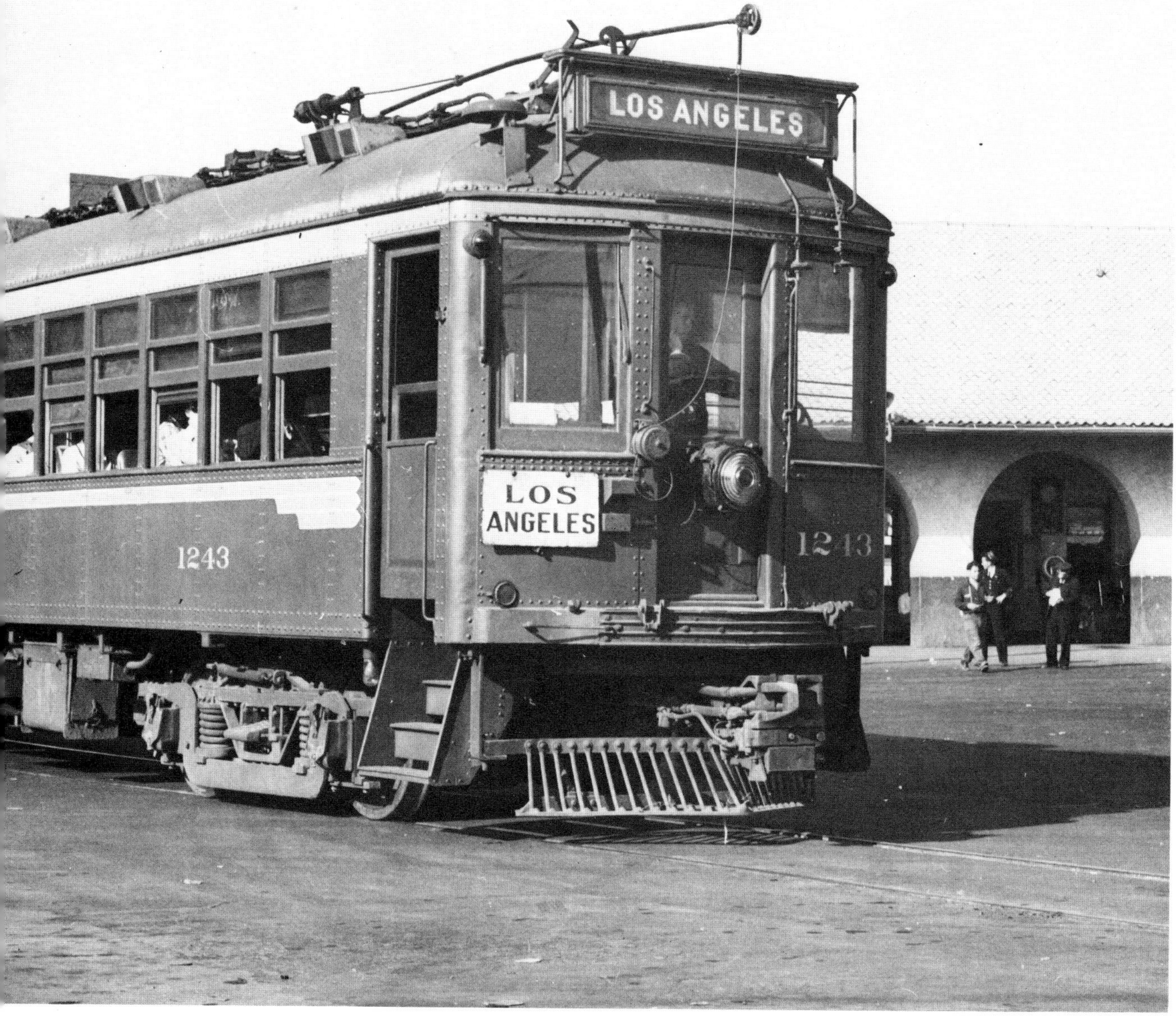

PACIFIC
ELECTRIC
WORLDS WONDERLAND LINES

PACIFIC
COMFORT - SPEED
- SAFETY -
ELECTRIC
WORLDS WONDERLAND LINES

PACIFIC
COMFORT - SPEED
- SAFETY -
ELECTRIC
WORLDS WONDERLAND LINES

RED CAR DAYS

Memories of the Pacific Electric

by Raphael F. Long

Interurbans Special 92

Interurban Press • Glendale, California

First Printing: Autumn 1983
ISBN 0-916374-63-7
Printed and bound in the United States of America

Published by
Interurban Press
P.O. Box 6444
Glendale, California 91205

Cover illustration by Roger Nannini

***Left:* With motors howling like banshees, a Venice Short Line train melds into a blur as it plummets through the Curson Curve. Minutes later, this journey toward the rising sun would culminate in the cavernous Hill Street Station.**

FOREWORD

Many years ago, far more than I really care to admit, a small boy developed a fascination and, yes, at times an obsession for a motley collection of old noisy decrepit red trolley cars belonging to an entity called "PE," whatever that meant. Slowly, as I grew, I made the observation that for some mysterious reason my beloved Red Cars were vanishing, never to be seen again. I didn't know how to stop or reverse the process, but in my young mind I knew I had to do something. It was then that I took an ancient box camera and started taking the pictures that are the basis of this album.

The photos herein came from the lenses of the god-awfullest collection of cameras, both box and bellows type, and all in 116/616-film size. The economics of picture taking 30-40 years ago dictated *cheap,* I mean *cheap!* I used outdated film at 15¢ a roll when and where I could find it. To further control costs, I never had anything printed—just developed. In fact, to this day (September 1983) I have thousands of negatives that have never been printed!

The style of railway photography has changed considerably over the years. Forty years ago it was the vogue to take close-cropped equipment shots with the sun at a very low angle so that the trucks and underframes were in detail. Large negatives up to post-card size were the rule to allow for the grain of those early films. Fixed shutter speeds of a fiftieth or hundredth of a second very effectively ruled out action shots. Color was available but it would last but a few years, then fade into a reddish-orange glob.

This album is an attempt to communicate some of the flavor of the Big Red Cars in their final years, to illustrate what they were like and to show some of the places they served. I hope this effort jars the memories of my contemporaries and enlightens those who came afterward.

I owe a special debt of gratitude to Interurban Press Publisher Mac Sebree for allowing me this forum; to Editor Jim Walker for his help and sage advice; and to Bill Bradley who formatted these pages.

I dedicate this effort to my wife Pat and my daughter Megan who gave me so much encouragement and help in putting it all together.

RED CAR DAYS

Not too many years ago, Southern California could boast of the "World's Largest Interurban Electric Railway System": the Pacific Electric and its Big Red Cars.

Pacific Electric was the southernmost in a chain of electric railway systems owned and operated by the Southern Pacific Railway.

Southern Pacific entered the local transportation picture around Los Angeles in 1903 with the acquisition of the Los Angeles Traction Company and its interurban subsidiary, California Pacific Railway. In 1906, SP acquired the Los Angeles-Pacific Company. This railway, known as the Balloon Route, served the western portion of Los Angeles County from downtown to the western beaches.

In 1910, SP purchased Henry Huntington's interests in a chain of electric railways in the four-county Los Angeles basin. These properties consisted of the *old* Pacific Electric, the Los Angeles Inter-Urban, the Los Angeles and Redondo, the Redlands Central, the San Bernardino Valley Traction, and the Riverside and Arlington. On September 1, 1911, Southern Pacific consolidated all of its Southern California holdings into one system, the *new* Pacific Electric. In 1912, PE acquired the Ontario and San Antonio Heights to round out its system.

After the Great Merger, PE embarked on a major program of reorganization and improvement. New lines were built to link up the isolated railways in San Bernardino and Riverside Counties. New cars were acquired and the famous red paint appeared on the cars throughout the system.

For the next 40 years Pacific Electric's Big Red Cars provided swift safe economical transportation to all of Southern California. The red trains went about everywhere. The lines extended along the beaches from Balboa to Santa Monica Canyon; from the cool snow-covered alpine heights of Mount Lowe to the hot dry sandy desert of the San Fernando Valley; and from urban downtown Los Angeles to the rural orange groves and vineyards of Orange, Riverside and San Bernardino Counties.

At its peak, Pacific Electric operated 6,200 trains daily over 1,061 miles of track.

During the era of the Red Cars, dramatic changes were taking place in this country. The local economy shifted from agricultural toward manufacturing; a terrible worldwide depression wrought unbelievable hardship; and a war of horrible dimensions followed. This, in turn, was followed by a period of unprecedented prosperity. All of these events were catalysts that brought about the massive use of automobiles and an almost national obsession for destroying, in the name of change, what our fathers and grandfathers had built, to be "modern." Freeways, urban renewal and the disposable society were born.

The decline of the Red Cars actually started in the 1920s when management began to realize that urban transport could be an extremely unprofitable and unrewarding enterprise. The Great Depression accelerated the decline. Marginal routes were converted to bus. Maintenance was deferred and schedules reduced to offset the massive hemorrhage of cash caused by the reduction of ridership.

In the period between 1937 and 1941, PE made a major effort to modernize the system. Unprofitable rail lines were abandoned and replaced by buses. Some bus operations were sold to other operators. The profitable rail lines were overhauled. Cars were refurbished and 30 new PCC streamliners acquired.

World War II caused an incredible renaissance of rail traffic, both passenger and freight. PE broke all prior records for the number of passengers carried and the tons of freight moved.

With the end of hostilities, the decline of the system resumed. After a vague attempt at modernization of the rail facilities, it was obvious that the prewar trend of declining patronage would continue. Between 1949 and 1951 the bulk of the remaining lines was either abandoned or converted to bus operation.

The Pacific Electric Railway as a passenger carrier passed away on October 1, 1953. For five years afterwards, its remaining lines were operated by Metropolitan Coach Lines, a company primarily interested in the operation of buses. In 1958, the dwindling lines were acquired by the state-owned Metropolitan Transit Authority, an agency ostensibly created to foster a mass transit system. It took this agency until April 8, 1961, to eliminate the last Pacific Electric rail passenger line. It is of note that the successors to the bureaucrats who did this want to spend 200 million-plus dollars of the taxpayers' money to restore the line to Long Beach that was so callously eliminated in the first place.

Meanwhile, Pacific Electric remained a freight carrier for many years, its big diesel locomotives chugging along the former passenger lines. On August 13, 1965, PE was merged into the Southern Pacific Railroad.

As Southern California's population density grows, a system similar to the PE will no doubt again serve the Southland. Today, the freeway system is approaching the gridlock stage where it will cease to function. The alternative is a surface rapid transit system not powered by fossil fuels. Unfortunately, if the bureaucrats have their way, it will be an absolute fiasco.

MAIN STREET STATION

1113 leads a three-car Santa Anita Race Track special down the ramp of the viaduct at San Pedro Street.

Owl-faced 1252 glides into Main Street traffic through the portal on the west side of the building. Originally, trains arrived and departed through this portal into a stub end track in the building. With construction of the elevated in 1917, departures such as this became rare. One exception was the annual Tournament of Roses Parade in Pasadena on New Year's Day.

Like some giant half wagon wheel, PE's lines radiated from Los Angeles to such diverse places as Pasadena on the north, San Bernardino-Riverside on the east and to Santa Ana, Long Beach and Balboa on the south. The absolute hub of this wheel was the big station at 6th and Main Streets.

When built in 1905, the Huntington Building (as it was originally called) was actually on the outskirts of town. The real center of commerce and government was in that area roughly confined by Alameda on the east, Third Street on the south, Figueroa on the west and Sunset on the north. Of course some of these places' names didn't apply back then. And no way geographically, topographically or sociologically did that Los Angeles of 1905 in any way resemble today's city. And that includes the so-called "restorations" around the plaza with the possible exception of the Pico House-Merced Theater complex.

Originally, the trains arrived and departed the station from a stub track in the Main Street side of the building. In 1914, a short elevated structure was added to the rear of the building. This provided storage space for trains between runs. The Southern District trains departed from a surface yard behind the station.

By 1917, traffic conditions on the streets around the terminal became unbearable. To provide some relief, the elevated structure was extended east to ground level at San Pedro Street. Trains then could enter and leave avoiding traffic in downtown proper.

Pacific Electric's offices were located in the building. Concourses for waiting, ticketing and boarding were on the second floor (main floor on Main Street side).

With minor exceptions, the building remained unchanged until the demise of the last Red Car line on April 8, 1961. Since then the elevated has been dismantled and the building relegated to that of a deteriorating old office building.

Long Beach-bound 303 departs over the 1917-built elevated extension. In 1911, rush hour Long Beach Flyers, departing from the surface terminal on ground level to the left of the picture, could cover the 20-mile-long line in 35 minutes. It is a little difficult to understand why, with 70-odd years of technical progress, this feat can't be equaled today.

The elevated station as it looked during the fall of 1950. There were few departures and arrivals at night which afforded this 30-second time exposure with ancient film and equally ancient camera.

THE SUBWAY TERMINAL

A whole generation has grown up without the slightest hint that at one time Los Angeles did have a subway.

During the first two decades of this century, traffic conditions in the downtown central city became unbelievably chaotic. Confusion reigned with an incredible mix of cars, pedestrians, horse-drawn vehicles, trolleys and jitneys.

Something had to be done and the city fathers did the only logical thing possible—they studied it. And when they completed one study, they started another. Finally when it became painfully obvious that the public sector couldn't get its act together, PE put out its own money and constructed the Subway Terminal to serve the western lines. (To be more specific, the lines to Beverly Hills, Hollywood, the San Fernando Valley and Glendale-Burbank used the new tunnel.)

The tunnel extended from a point near Glendale and Beverly Boulevards under Bunker Hill to a five-track stub terminal near Fifth and Hill Streets. The new station was in the basement of the height-limit Subway Terminal Building. The Subway opened on December 1, 1925.

The Hill Street Station, a surface terminal, was located immediately south of the Subway Terminal Building. This served the Venice, Redondo and Santa Monica lines as it had from the first decade of this century. It also served as a storage yard for the little Echo Park Avenue cars.

For the next 30 years, the subway, though a modest one mile in length, did a magnificent job of reducing surface traffic in the central city. Unfortunately, it fell victim to our love affair with the automobile. The subway era ended in Los Angeles on June 19, 1955, with the passing of the Glendale-Burbank line.

The original subway cost five million dollars for one mile in 1925 dollars. Today's planned Metro Rail will cost an estimated 166 million dollars a mile in 1985 dollars.

A Glendale civic group poses for the obligatory photograph before boarding the first train to carry passengers from the new Subway Terminal. The date was November 30, 1925, the day before commencement of regular service. This car type, known as a "Big Five," was used until the late thirties.

Photograph from Security First National Bank Collection

Opposite page: **The tunnel as viewed from the base of the interlocking plant far below Olive Street. Despite the water-marks on the walls, the tunnel was surprisingly dry. The little recesses for the lights afforded refuge from passing trains while walking through the tunnel; an act which the railway didn't condone.**

Left: Santa Monica Boulevard car 659 plunges through the tunnel portal and 120 seconds later will be in the underground terminal. The building on the left was the electrical substation for the whole tunnel complex, and the switch at the right led to Toluca yard, a small car storage facility just outside the portal. Beverly Boulevard crosses over Glendale Boulevard on the bridge in the background.

Below: Looking into the stub terminal during the construction phase of 1925. Movement of cars into the station was controlled from the interlocking tower in the center of the photo.

Photograph from the Security First National Bank Collection

A Hollywood Boulevard car prepares to depart from Track Five.

An old gateman would bellow, as he opened the steel mesh gates in the terminal mezzanine, "Board Glendale and North Glendale, Edendale, Atwater and all local stops." And that's exactly what those people milling around the platform intended to do in this view of North Glendale-bound 5025.

ARCHITECTURE

Much, if not most, of the construction of electric railways around Southern California was done in conjunction with real estate development. In 1900, most of what is now Los Angeles, Orange, Riverside and San Bernardino counties was wide-open spaces. Potential buyers demanded the availability of inexpensive, reliable transportation. In many instances, the railway was also the land developer or in partnership with a developer. To convey the image of quality and permanence, impressive stations were erected.

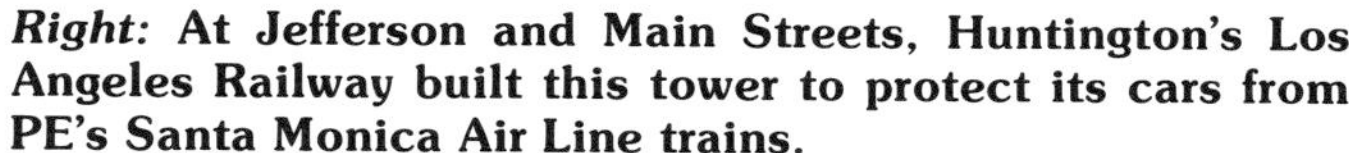

Right: **At Jefferson and Main Streets, Huntington's Los Angeles Railway built this tower to protect its cars from PE's Santa Monica Air Line trains.**

Below: **The Ivy power substation was located on Venice Boulevard in Culver City. This was a good example of the California Mission-style architecture most commonly used.**

Top: The Oneonta Park station and tower at Fair Oaks Avenue and Huntington Drive in South Pasadena illustrates California Mission architecture as practiced in 1902. It was a wood frame structure covered with plaster and could easily have complied with today's stringent building codes.

Right: The Playa Del Rey power substation and waiting room was done in California Gold Rush style. With broad roof and narrow windows, all it lacked was iron shutters. This building fell into disuse with the discontinuance of the Redondo via Del Rey line on May 12, 1940, and was demolished in the fifties. Like so many early structures, this one was of un-reinforced masonry. One major earthquake and it could become a tomb for anyone inside.

Bottom: When Southern Pacific became firmly entrenched in the driver's seat, it became low tide at finance pier as witnessed by this standardized and very austere station in Huntington Beach.

The dash sign rack at Macy Street Yard gave a clear indication of those lines still in operation during the Northern District's final years.

Above: Macy Street Carhouse was located adjacent to the Ramona (San Bernardino) Freeway on the west side of Los Angeles County Hospital and Poor Farm. This was the primary storage and service for the Northern District interurban cars.

Below left: The electric substation and cooling tower at Newport Beach.

Below right: Automatic crossing gates, with but two exceptions, were nonexistent on the Pacific Electric. This wigwag installation at Chandler Boulevard and Ethel Avenue in Van Nuys was typical of those used throughout the system. Needless to say, grade crossing accidents were many. In an effort to reduce these accidents, the company instructed its motormen to come to an almost complete stop at each crossing. The net result was a game of "chicken" between trains and automobiles. There were probably just as many accidents and a lot fewer riders because the schedules were slowed down.

LINES OF THE PACIFIC ELECTRIC RAILWAY IN SOUTHERN CALIFORNIA

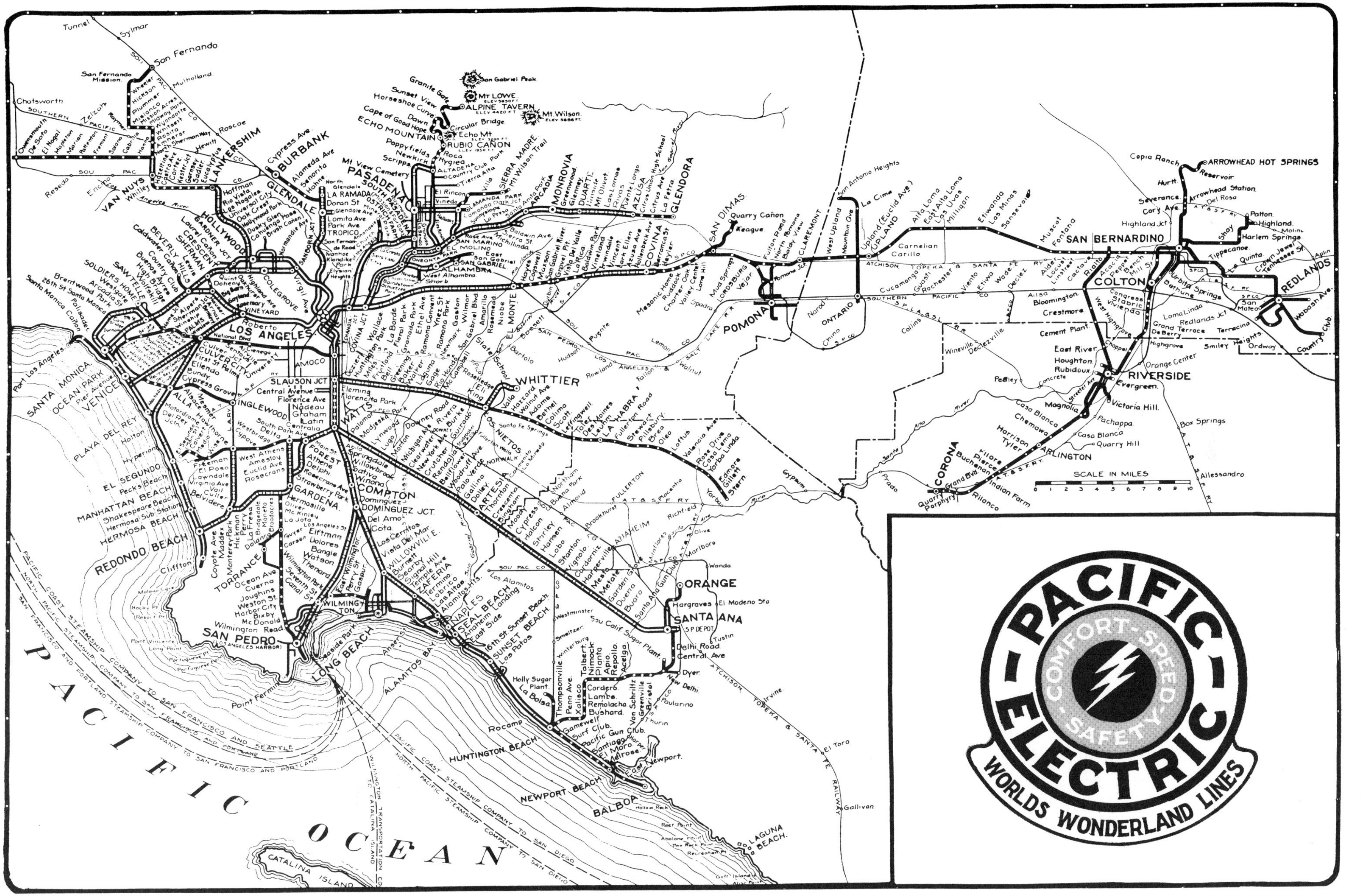

PACIFIC ELECTRIC
COMFORT · SPEED · SAFETY
WORLDS WONDERLAND LINES

SCALE IN MILES
0 1 2 3 4 5 6 7 8 9 10

PACIFIC OCEAN

LOS ANGELES
PASADENA
SOUTH PASADENA
ALHAMBRA
GLENDALE
BURBANK
LANKERSHIM
VAN NUYS
HOLLYWOOD
SHERMAN
SAWTELLE
SANTA MONICA
OCEAN PARK
VENICE
PLAYA DEL REY
EL SEGUNDO
MANHATTAN BEACH
HERMOSA BEACH
REDONDO BEACH
TORRANCE
GARDENA
SAN PEDRO
WILMINGTON
LONG BEACH
NAPLES
SEAL BEACH
SUNSET BEACH
HUNTINGTON BEACH
NEWPORT BEACH
BALBOA
LAGUNA BEACH
SANTA ANA
ORANGE
ANAHEIM
FULLERTON
LA HABRA
WHITTIER
COMPTON
WATTS
INGLEWOOD
CULVER CITY
EL MONTE
COVINA
SAN GABRIEL
ARCADIA
MONROVIA
AZUSA
GLENDORA
SIERRA MADRE
ALPINE TAVERN
MT LOWE
Mt Wilson
ECHO MOUNTAIN
RUBIO CAÑON
SAN DIMAS
POMONA
CLAREMONT
UPLAND
ONTARIO
SAN BERNARDINO
COLTON
REDLANDS
RIVERSIDE
ARLINGTON
CORONA
ARROWHEAD HOT SPRINGS
CATALINA ISLAND

PACIFIC COAST STEAMSHIP COMPANY TO SAN FRANCISCO AND SEATTLE
NORTH PACIFIC STEAMSHIP COMPANY TO SAN FRANCISCO AND PORTLAND
SAN FRANCISCO AND PORTLAND STEAMSHIP COMPANY TO SAN FRANCISCO AND PORTLAND
WILMINGTON TRANSPORTATION CO TO CATALINA ISLAND
PACIFIC COAST STEAMSHIP COMPANY TO SAN DIEGO
NORTH PACIFIC STEAMSHIP COMPANY TO SAN DIEGO
ATCHISON TOPEKA & SANTA FE RAILWAY
SOUTHERN PACIFIC

SAN FERNANDO VALLEY
SANTA MONICA BLVD.
CAHUENGA PASS
UNIVERSAL CITY
NORTH HOLLYWOOD
VAN NUYS
5170

CITY AND SUBURBAN

Prior to 1922, Pacific Electric's city and suburban service was provided by an unbelievably diverse collection of cars which for the most part were acquired in the Great Merger of 1911.

This equipment required an enormous spare parts inventory to support. Shop personnel had to be highly skilled and the shops made capable to rebuild or remanufacture anything. The riding public was none too thrilled with these cars which for the most part were slow, noisy and had open-air sections which were fine in the summer but terribly uncomfortable during the wet winter season.

To correct these deficiencies, PE contracted with the St. Louis Car Company for 50 center-entrance steel cars which arrived on the property commencing in 1922. From their first appearance in a parade on Hollywood Boulevard, these cars, numbered in the 600 series, gained wide public approval. The company was so satisfied with them that they ordered three additional lots from St. Louis Car and the J.G. Brill Company until the fleet grew to a total of 160 cars by 1928.

Named "Hollywoods" for the busiest of all city-suburban lines, they became the backbone of the car fleet until the demise of those lines in the 1950s.

Unfortunately these cars possessed two major design flaws which were to haunt them throughout their existence. Having four 45-hp motors, they had a top speed of only 28 mph when first delivered. The location of the trucks prevented installation of double front doors so necessary for viable one-man operation. Simply stated, these cars were too slow to maintain competitive schedules and required too much labor to operate economically.

To remedy these deficiencies, PE undertook to rewind the motors of the entire fleet during the great modernization of 1939-41. The Eclipse fenders were removed and skirting applied. New seating and lighting was applied to the interior and a new paint scheme modeled on SP's Daylight motif was applied. Despite these improvements, the cars were still limited to 45 mph tops.

In 1949, 131 cars were rebuilt for one-man service. The horizontal guillotine center doors were replaced with folding-type doors and air treadle door actuators were installed; there was no way to correct the single front entrance door. During this remodeling, these cars were renumbered from the 600-700 series to the new 5050 series which immediately earned the unfortunate nickname of "Hermaphrodites."

As the red car lines were discontinued during the fifties, these cars were sold or scrapped. Several survive today at the Orange Empire Railway Museum at Perris, California.

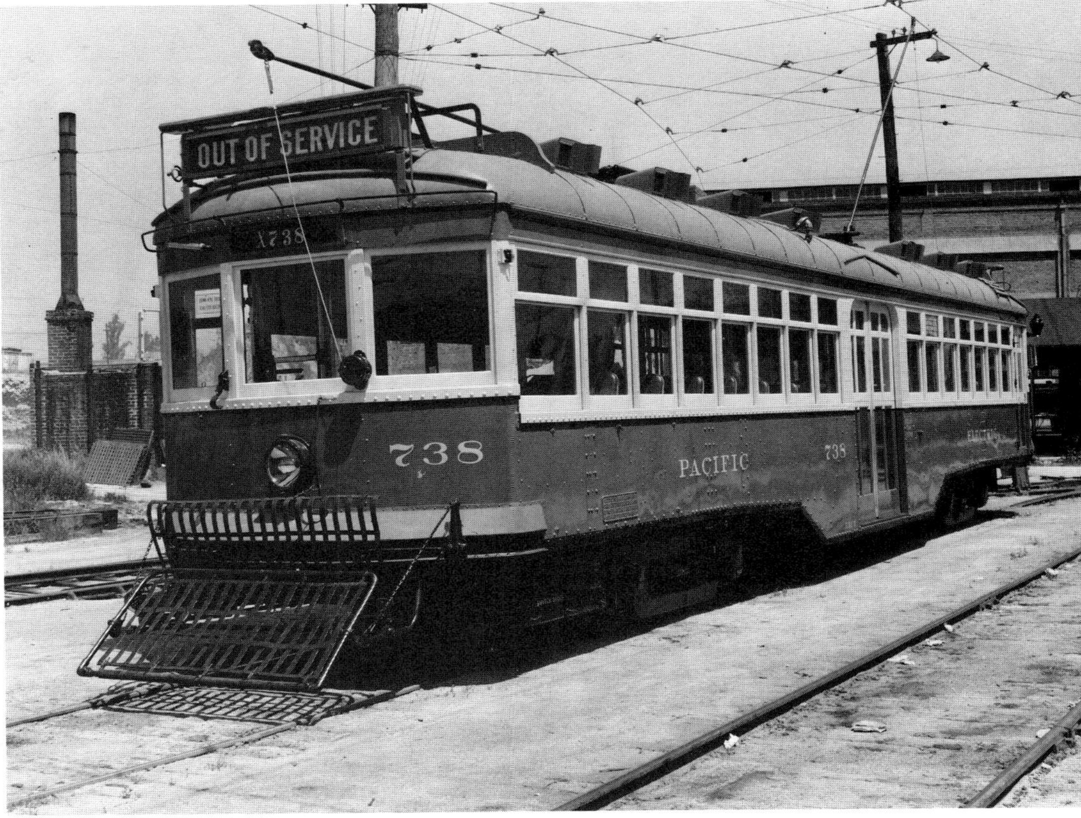

Right: **With the exception of the overhead roller sign and the red, cream and black paint scheme, 738 models the original appearance of these cars. This 1938 photo was taken at Sherman immediately after the car had undergone upgrading for use on the San Fernando Valley lines.** ***Arrow Studios photo from Jeff Moreau***

Opposite page: **5170 paused briefly in front of the North Hollywood station for this picture.**

Two San Fernando Valley trains pass at Universal City station in the median strip of the Cahuenga Freeway, in 1951. The barren hill on the left was the location for many "oater" and "sci-fi" epics from the early Hollywood era. Today it is the site of Universal Studios and a major high-rise complex.

Subway-bound 5140 pauses briefly at Sanborn Junction (Sunset and Santa Monica Boulevards). There are 48 stars on the flag in this 1953 view. The car on the left is a 1949 Mercury convertible. The dash sign was red with white letters.

There were two segments of four-track right-of-way on the Pacific Electric System. One, on the north, extended five and a half miles along Huntington Drive between Indian Village and El Molino. Local passenger and freight trains used the outer set of tracks; the center tracks were reserved for limiteds. *Above:* Los Angeles-bound 1133 passes the small storage yard just west of Sierra Vista. *Below:* Photographing the PE wasn't always a piece of cake. During both World War II and the Korean War there were scares about "fifth columnists" and "saboteurs" taking pictures of our nation's industrial and transportation facilities. There were citizens lurking everywhere eager to apprehend these marauders. This photograph on the four track through El Serreno was taken seconds before I was approached by two minions of the law who informed me that they had a call about someone hanging like a bat from one of the catenary towers taking pictures. At this point in time my camera was neatly folded in my hip pocket. Since I was wearing a bright red track walker's tunic and obviously belonged there, "Would I keep an eye open for this evildoer?"

Cahuenga Pass is the gateway between Hollywood and the San Fernando Valley. The Los Angeles Pacific Company started construction of the rail line through the Pass in 1911, completed by the post-merger PE. The San Fernando Valley line extended to Van Nuys (Sherman Way and Van Nuys Boulevard) where it forked into two branches. One of these extended to the city of San Fernando via Van Nuys Blvd., Parthenia Street, Sepulveda and Brand Boulevards, while the other headed due west on Sherman Way to Owensmouth (Canoga Park). In the view above, we see the Pass as it looked in 1922. This panorama remained relatively unchanged until construction of the Cahuenga Freeway in 1939. The eucalyptus trees were near the site of the present-day Mulholland overpass. *Photograph from the Security First National Bank Collection. Below:* Three Hollywood Bowl Special trains wait to take the Pilgrimage Bridge cross-over. I was standing on what is now the fast lane of the Hollywood Freeway when this picture was taken.

This 1951 photo, taken from the grove of tall trees seen in the earlier view on the preceding page, shows the expanse of the Cahuenga Freeway. This short section of grade-separated median and the short downtown subway was as close as Los Angeles came to rail rapid transit.

Heading for Los Angeles, 5179 passes under Barham Boulevard - Dark Canyon Road.

"Hollywood" car 5155 prepares to depart Sherman Way and Van Nuys Boulevard for the 89-minute trek to Los Angeles. In an earlier time, this was the junction between the Owensmouth (Canoga Park) line along Sherman Way and the line to the City of San Fernando.

Van Nuys-bound 5156 races up Vineland Avenue and across the north channel bridge over the Los Angeles River. This site is now buried 30 feet under the Hollywood Freeway! I remember during the floods of 1938 when this area was the scene of almost total destruction with many homes completely undermined by the flow of water through this wash. The Army Corps of Engineers concreted in the main channel to the south and this tributary became a dry wash. Watercress grew in abundance along the riverbed and many times I recall hiking out behind Republic Studios to collect it.

The Sherman Barn at West Hollywood was home base for the Western District lines.

A lineup of maintenance-of-way equipment at Sherman. Rail grinder 00199 was formerly passenger car 1001. Wrecker 005 can be seen directly behind her. To the right is 00164, the only tower car that would fit through the Subway tunnel.

THE STREAMLINERS

Pacific Electric's PCC streamliners were born of compromise. In the late 1930s, PE petitioned the California Railroad Commission for permission to substitute bus for rail services over a very large part of the system. In exchange for permission to do this, PE would purchase 30 new PCC streamliners for the Venice Short Line. Under the plan, all of the remaining wooden passenger cars would be removed from service by the end of 1940.

St. Louis Car Company was approached with a proposal to build a double-ended PCC with multiple unit control so that they could be operated in three-car trains. St. Louis flat out said *no!* The concept of the PCC was one standard, single-ended car and the operator of that design would change his facility to accommodate the car rather than the car to the facility.

Undaunted by this rejection, PE management approached the Pullman-Standard Car Manufacturing Company of Worcester, Mass. In short order, 30 new cars arrived on the property.

The new cars were assigned to two lines: one a consolidation of the Hollywood Boulevard and Venice Short Line and the other to Glendale-Burbank.

Problems with the new cars developed from the start. At 42 mph, the PCCs were slower than the 950s they were replacing. They also tended to gallop on the Short Line's rough track and their motors tended to overheat during sustained running. The civil defense authorities ordered that the roofs of the cars be repainted from silver to a less reflective cocoa.

Eventually all these cars were reassigned to the more docile Glendale-Burbank line where they functioned very well. They were quiet and accelerated rapidly. Most important of all, they were very popular with the riding public.

After cessation of the Glendale line in 1955, the PCCs were sold to the General Urquiza Railway of Buenos Aires, Argentina. They were not too successful in their new environment and were scrapped shortly thereafter.

***Left:* A group of PCCs in the Burbank yard which was located on the south side of Glenoaks Boulevard between Orange Grove and Palm Avenues.**

***Below:* Subway Terminal-bound 5011 passes the car storage yards on Glenoaks Boulevard between Central and Pacific Avenues in Glendale.**

Hollywood Boulevard 5020 poses in this 1949 view at First and Hill Streets. You're looking west toward Court Hill on the right and Bunker Hill on the left. Downtown Los Angeles was a fascinating place to visit before the advent of freeways and urban renewal.

A railfans' excursion brought 5028 to the freight-only Whittier line. The company didn't relish chartering these cars out over foreign lines. A mechanical failure could have caused a major disruption of service with no way to retrieve the car because of dissimilar coupler heights. On two charters using these cars, there were grade crossing accidents because motorists didn't recognize the unique air horns used on the PCCs.

TUNNELS

The complex of tunnels in these two views was built by the Los Angeles Pacific Company for their lines to Hollywood. When opened on September 15, 1909, they eliminated a tortuous and time-consuming route through old central Los Angeles.

Left: **We are looking north from Temple and Hill Streets at the northerly tunnel, which extended through Fort Moore Hill to Sunset Boulevard. During the early fifties the hill was removed and the site became part of the downtown slot of the Hollywood Freeway.**

Below: **Looking south from almost the same point we see the twin bores of the south tunnel, which ran through Court Hill. Until the very early forties, Court Flight, a small funicular railway, extended from Broadway up this hill to a point behind the building on top of the hill (at left in the photo). Court Hill is gone now; gone right down to street level and the location is filled with government buildings.**

Car 110 prepares to turn onto Echo Park Avenue from Sunset Boulevard. St. Louis Car Company built 15 of these cars for PE in 1930. They were equipped with four 35-hp motors and had a top speed of 28 mph. After the demise of the Echo Park Avenue line, in 1950, these cars were sold to Vera Cruz, Mexico.

Wire greaser 00150 performs her weekly chore along Hollywood Boulevard. Built in 1899 by the Los Angeles Pacific Company, she survives today in the collection of the Orange Empire Railway Museum at Perris, California. That's Sid Grauman's Chinese Theatre on the left and hidden behind the palm trees is the Hollywood Hotel, a landmark that has long since perished.

WOODEN CARS

Two classes of wooden interurban cars survived well into the final decade of Pacific Electric's passenger operations. It wasn't planned that way, but events conspired to keep them around 10 years past their scheduled retirement.

As part of the great system modernization of 1939-41, all wooden passenger cars were to be scrapped. The abandonment of such lines as Redondo Beach, Temple City, Balboa, Santa Monica via Beverly Hills and the Brentwood-San Vicente line plus the acquisition of 30 new PCC streamliners was supposed to free up enough steel cars to allow for retirement of all remaining woods.

Two events occurred that saved the "woods" for those 10 years. First, the PCCs that were to replace the 950s simply couldn't perform in a reasonable manner. The other mitigating circumstance was the Japanese bombing of Pearl Harbor which immediately caused the remaining 1000 series to be pulled out of the scrap lines, repainted and returned to service.

The 950s were constructed in 1907 for the Los Angeles-Pacific Company (or Balloon Route as early Angelenos were so fond of calling it). Their initial assignment was on the Venice and Sawtelle lines. They were designed for sustained running in a proposed Vineyard Subway between downtown Fifth and Hill Streets and a point near Fourth and Vermont Streets but a major recession in 1907 killed the subway plan. Thus, these cars were condemned to a lifetime of operation over congested downtown city streets.

Rapid acceleration was not one of their virtues. Four 75-hp motors gave them a top speed of 47 mph. They weighed in at 78,900 pounds.

With the merger of the Los Angeles-Pacific into the Pacific Electric system in 1911, the 950s were reassigned to the Pasadena lines. The arrival of the 1100 series in 1924 resulted in their return to their original haunts.

During and after World War II, the 950s were used on the Venice Short Line and the once-a-day Santa Monica Air Line. The 1000s shared these assignments and also served the Long Beach-San Pedro via West Basin line. During the racing season, the 1000s operated to the Santa Anita Race Track at Arcadia.

On Sunday, September 17, 1950, buses replaced the Venice Short Line. The remaining 950s and 1000s were promptly consigned to the scrapper's torch at National Steel and Metal on Terminal Island.

***Above:* Car 955 leads a three-car train west on the San Vicente Line at the Pico Boulevard overpass while deadheading to the Sherman Barn at West Hollywood.**

Two views of 988. The one above is at the Hill Street Station and the other is in front of Sherman Barn at West Hollywood. These pictures illustrate that these cars were not symmetrical, a holdover from the days when one end was open and devoid of windows. The upper photo was taken by the late Robert Loewing.

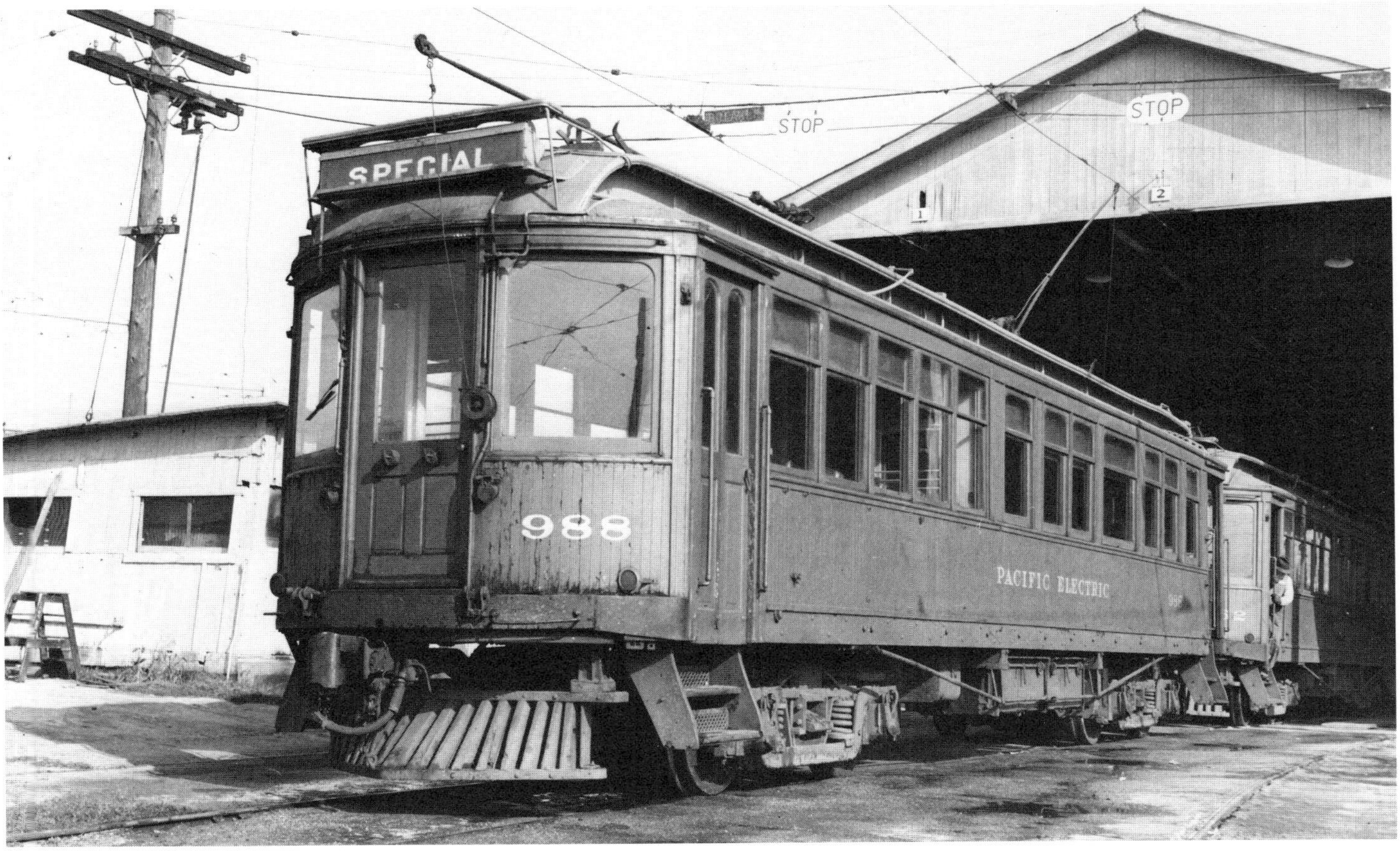

Left: **Car 999 was the only 950 to have a five-window end. This car was the parlor car "El Viento" (The Wind) and her one great claim to fame was in transporting President Taft to the Old Soldiers' Home at Sawtelle in 1910.**

965 leads a three-car train up Hill Street just north of Fifth Street, a common sight during rush hours for most of the first half of this century. This was also the "Achilles' heel" of Pacific Electric. Had there been truly free access into and out of the central urban core to the suburban private rights-of-way, the PE system might have survived to this day. Admittedly, it would have been under the auspices of some public entity, and yes, it was a public entity that dealt the *coup de grace* to the last remaining PE line in 1961.

Above: Car 981 and train southbound on Trolley Way at Bicknell Street. This right-of-way extended along the beach from Santa Monica to Venice. The ornate little waiting shelter was a holdover from the Los Angeles-Pacific days.

Below: The Ocean Park carhouse was located on Trolley Way midway between Santa Monica and Venice. The building was considered a serious fire hazard. It was of wood frame construction sheathed with one-by-twelves. The cars stored there were also wood. The railway personnel were extremely intolerant of visitors, particularly those who might be careless with fire. Smoking was forbidden around this facility.

Car 1012 poses in the Saturday morning sun at Ocean Park Substation. This car had drawn the once-a-weekday Santa Monica Air Line franchise run. The Air Line was the backbone of PE's Western District freight operations and the franchise that granted PE the right to use certain parts of this line stipulated that there be passenger service of a minimum of one round trip per weekday. Though never advertised, the Air Line enjoyed a following of about 50 commuters who rode year after year.

Newport Beach-bound 1044 pauses briefly at Huntington Beach. The cushioning effect of the drifting sand which covered the tracks rendered passing trains almost noiseless. Trainmen had to be extremely cautious because beachgoers were constantly walking in front of their trains. Tin Can Beach, famous for its accumulation of beer cans, can be seen in the distance. Today, both the railway and the cans are gone, victims of change.

For scenic beauty, I had three favorite PE lines: Glendora, San Fernando Valley and Newport-Balboa.

Left: Newport Beach-bound 1044 crosses the Alamitos Bay bridge at low tide.

Below: Former Peninsular Railway of San Jose 1053, with a waggish Echo Park Avenue on the destination sign, pauses momentarily at Vineyard Junction. It was here at Vineyard, on July 13, 1913, that two three-car trains of wooden cars collided. Twelve people were killed and over 200 injured. The 1000 series was in the process of fabrication at the builders, Jewett Car Company, when the tragedy occurred. The accident branded every wood car obsolete.

The Tens were equipped with four 100-hp motors and were capable of speeds up to 60 mph. They could be operated on both 600 and 1200-volt current. These cars opened the San Bernardino line in 1914. Their tenure on that line was short; by 1915 they were replaced by the then-new, all-steel 1200 series. For the rest of their service life the Tens played a secondary role to the steel cars.

SPECIAL
SANTA -
- ANITA
RACE TRACK
1123

THE BIG SUBURBANS

Pacific Electric operated two classes of all-metal cars which were truly *The Big Red Cars.* The 1100 series provided the short-haul suburban service and the 1200 series was the long-haul interurbans.

The Elevens were a design compromise between the 1200 series which predated them by nine years and Southern Pacific's San Francisco Bay suburban cars. Their carbodies were almost identical to the Twelves with the notable exception of double entrance steps similar to the San Francisco Bay cars. Of course the trucks and running gear were state-of-the-art 1924.

Fifty cars were built by the Standard Steel Car Company. Each car weighed in at 96,700 pounds. Four 110-hp motors gave them a top speed of 50 mph. These machines were equipped for use on 600-volt current only; thus, they could not be used on the 1200-volt line to San Bernardino.

The Elevens were assigned principally to the Pasadena, Sierra Madre and Monrovia-Glendora lines on the Northern District, and some saw service to Santa Ana and Long Beach on the Southern District.

The Elevens were fun to ride. They could get up and move almost effortlessly. They were solidly built. There was no deflection in the carbody and no rattle even on the roughest track. There was an interesting sidelight brought about by the double step arrangement. To clear the steps, the carbuilder located the trucks closer to the center of the car. This resulted in one wheel set from each truck striking rail joints simultaneously. Thus, an Eleven could be recognized by a unique "clop-clop" sound. They also tended to gallop rather than rock on PE's rough and decrepit track.

In 1951, with the abandonment of the Northern District lines, these cars became surplus. They were sold to the General Urquiza Railway of Buenos Aires, Argentina, where they saw many more years of service.

Below: **1127 basks in the afternoon sun at the Sierra Madre Station. The descent down the hill to San Marino would be rapid that afternoon during the summer of 1950. A few short months later, this line would be no more.**

Opposite page: **Closeup view of the business end of 1123 as she lays over at Macy Street Yard. During the racing season, a ride to Santa Anita at Arcadia was a full speed and few stops adventure. The big signs on the front of all PE cars left no doubt as to their destinations.**

Above: **Side by side on the elevated platform at Main Street Station are 1121 and former San Francisco East Bay car 411.**

Below: **1128 leads a three-car deadhead movement south on San Pedro Street between Fifth and Sixth Streets. This section of line was a PE-watcher's paradise with cars moving in both directions at less than one-minute intervals. And if one waited long enough, he or she would see almost every piece of PE rolling stock assigned to the North.**

Above: **1122 appears to be going the wrong way in this view at East Duarte on the Glendora line. Actually the line was single track with one very long passing siding. The Glendora route was one of the more scenic lines with ample vistas of orange groves, small farms and the ever majestic San Gabriel mountains.**

Right: **Pasadena Oak Knoll 1110 rounds the hill behind the Huntington Hotel.**

1101 and 1119 cross Sawpit Wash near Azusa on a very smoggy morning dash for Los Angeles.

During an excursion, 1100 pauses for the photographer in this October 15, 1950, view taken along Santa Ana's Fourth Street.

THE BIG INTERURBANS

The "Twelve Hundreds" were the finest cars PE ever owned. They provided the backbone of interurban operations on the main lines to San Bernardino, Long Beach and Santa Ana.

There were three major variants of this class: the *San Bernardino, Long Beach* and *Portlands*. In addition there was a subvariant of the San Bernardino called the *Butterfly*.

All motor cars could be operated together indiscriminately; they all possessed the same control systems. All were equipped with four 140-hp motors and all were capable of operation on either 600 or 1200-volt current.

The first lot of cars to operate on the PE was constructed in 1915 for the then newly opened San Bernardino line. Built by Pressed Steel Car Company, these cars weighed 109,200 pounds. They were capable of 60-mph speeds. Numbered 1200 through 1221, they were known as the *San Bernardino Twelves*.

In 1921, the Pullman Company built an additional 30 cars. Twenty of these were motors and 10 trailers. These units were virtually identical to the earlier Twelves with two notable exceptions: the motor cars were geared lower to permit better acceleration while pulling trailers (or "sleds" as they were called). This had the effect of lowering their top speed to 55 mph. Having been designed for the relatively short Long Beach line, they were not fitted with lavatories. This upped their seating capacity to 64 over the San Bernardino's 60.

The *Long Beach Twelves* were 1,120 pounds lighter than their earlier sisters. The motor cars in this group were numbered 1222 through 1241 and the trailers 1242 through 1251.

The final lot of Twelves arrived on the Pacific Electric property in 1928. These cars were acquired second-hand from the Portland, Eugene and Eastern Railway, another SP subsidiary. Twelve cars became 1252 through 1263. One car became business car 1299.

Long Beach 1243 poses at the San Bernardino Station during a railfans' excursion. This car was originally built as a trailer; a sister car was demolished in a wreck and 1243 received that car's motors and electrical equipment.

The *Portlands* were the oldest, having been built by Pullman in 1912. They served as the pattern for the first PE Twelves that followed three years later. At 102,400 pounds, they were the lightest. The principal differences between the *Portlands* and the other PE Twelves were their red, green and gold leaded glass upper side windows and their owl-like porthole end windows. They were also the fastest with 70-mph speeds possible during sustained running.

During the great modernization of the system in 1939 a subvariant of the San Bernardino Twelves appeared. Six cars were upgraded for improved San Bernardino service. The major changes consisted of improved interior lighting and seating. A very striking paint scheme was applied to the exterior consisting of the basic red with bright orange "butterflies."

The Twelves were very substantially constructed. This was particularly true with the San Bernardino and Long Beach types. They were very comfortable to ride, reliable to operate and suffered few mechanical failures.

The arrival of the "Blimps" sounded the death knell for these cars. They were bumped off the Long Beach, San Pedro and Santa Ana lines by the bigger cars and they survived only until the abandonment of the Baldwin Park turnback of the San Bernardino line on October 14, 1950. PE sought buyers for these cars but found none. In April of 1951 they were sold to the Kaiser Steel Corporation at Fontana, California, where they were scrapped.

Only one of these cars survives today. Business car 1299 was sold to private individuals for preservation.

***Below:* *San Bernardino* 1201 sits in the warm summer sun on the viaduct of Main Street Station. A few minutes after this picture was taken, she boarded her passengers for the run to Baldwin Park.**

1220 shows off her bright orange "butterflies" at Seventh Street Surface Yard. The red and orange color scheme had its origins in parent company Southern Pacific's *Coast Daylight* streamliners.

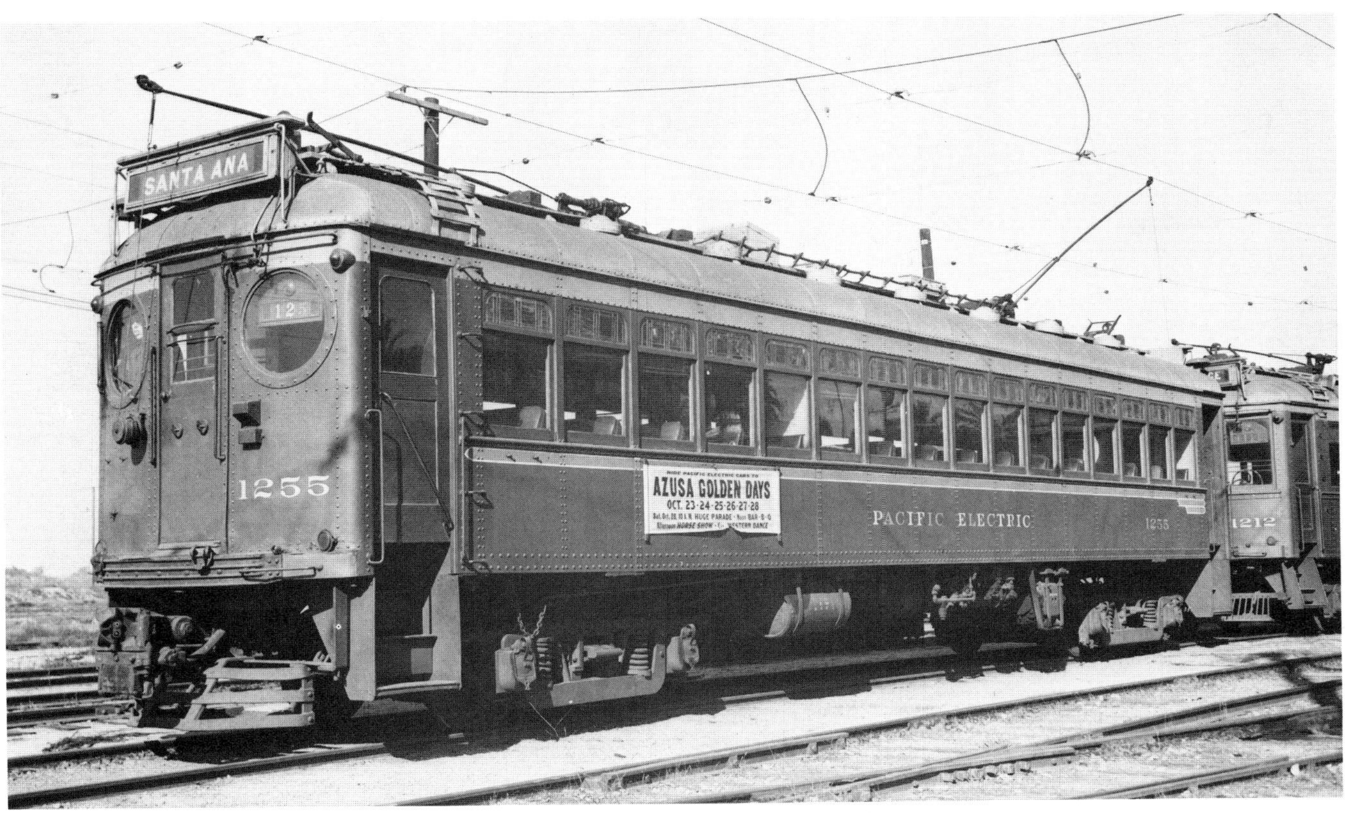

The yellow, green and red leaded glass upper sash are very evident in this picture of *Portland* car 1255. The locale is Fairbanks Yard at Long Beach.

During a three-week period each September, special trains were operated to the Los Angeles County Fairgrounds at Pomona. The Ramona (now San Bernardino) Freeway hadn't even reached Eastern Avenue and you could average no more than 30 mph over the roads in the San Gabriel Valley. The big red trains were the fastest way to get to the fair. It was always hot and humid with the fall winds churning up the fine dust of the Pomona Valley. A mixture of the sweet aroma of orange blossoms and the pungent aroma of cattle manure filled the air. With "Covina" rolled on her destination sign, Long Beach 1234 awaits that evening's return trip.

Left: Torrance Shops was the repository for the Long Beach "Sleds" during the years following World War II.

Above: **Pomona-bound "Portland" 1260 pauses briefly for orders at La Verne before continuing to the Los Angeles County Fairgrounds.**

Below: **Two "Portland" combination passenger-express cars are coupled back to back near Torrance. With the urbanization of Southern California, such scenes of desolation are gone.**

1299

Business car 1299 was the most traveled car on the whole Pacific Electric system. She was fitted with kitchen, lavatory and conference tables. Her interior was carpeted and filled with big comfortable leather chairs. She even had "trips" to allow her to be operated into the subway. Her end windows were cut down to afford better visibility during inspection tours which were made at least once a week.

PE management knew something that has been "unlearned" by management throughout America today. They would go out and inspect the property, visit the shops and talk to the people who made the whole thing go. Their decisions were thus based on firsthand information rather than relying on manipulated data from some middle manager.

A lot of the decisions these men made were unpopular. I know; I didn't like a lot of them. But they had the courage of their convictions to make honest decisions based on fact. They were real managers in every sense of the word.

A San Bernardino-bound freight passes 1299 at LaVerne; the business car had been backed into the "hole" to allow the longer freight to pass.

Alamitos Bay, at high tide, is the setting for this view of Los Angeles-bound 1299 on the Newport-Balboa line. The only revenue service this car performed was as club car COMMODORE to Balboa. I recall crossing this trestle one foggy morning to find it crawling with 50 to 75 fishermen who had but one place to go: over the side! ***Photograph by Fred Matthews***

The deluxe business car basks in the afternoon sun on Rialto's Riverside Avenue. The white sidewalls are very evident against the Pullman-green truck frames.

1299, with PCC 5015 and New York City Fifth Avenue Coach Company 1212, lines up at Brand Boulevard and Mountain Avenue in North Glendale. I enjoyed the dubious distinction of being one of the four owners of the bus.

THE BLIMPS

The *Blimps* were the largest interurban cars operated by the Pacific Electric. They also comprised the total interurban fleet during the last 10 years of red car service in Southern California.

These cars were brought to PE by the United States Maritime Commission at the onset of World War II. They were first used to transport war workers over a newly built branch line to the Calship yards at Terminal Island. As with everything that government does, there was an excess of cars for the Calship Specials, so the cars were utilized on other PE routes as well. With a shortage of its own equipment, PE was able to eventually buy all of these cars from the government. At the end of the war, PE elected to refurbish and renumber most of them.

Cars numbered into the 400 series came from the Interurban Electric Railway, a Southern Pacific subsidiary which served the San Francisco East Bay area. These cars were built by the American Car and Foundry in 1911 and by the Pullman Company in 1913. They weighed 115,840 pounds each and had a top speed of about 45 mph.

The 300 series, although almost identical in appearance to the 400s, was constructed in 1929 and 1930 by the St. Louis Car Company. Before coming to the PE, these cars were fixtures on another SP electric line, the Northwestern Pacific, a line serving Marin County on the north side of San Francisco bay. These cars weighed 110,200 pounds. They were lighter than the 400s because they were built of a combination of aluminum and steel. They were faster than the East Bay cars, with a top speed of 50 mph.

PE used the *Blimps* on the lines to Glendora, Santa Ana, Long Beach and San Pedro.

These cars, though slower and mechanically inferior to PE's Elevens and Twelves, carried 25 percent more passengers. Simple economics dictated that these cars would outlast the others.

As each remaining Red Car line was abandoned, small groups of these cars were scrapped. Finally, with the demise of the Long Beach line on April 8, 1961, all the remaining cars were scrapped. Several examples survive today, most notably in the collection of the Orange Empire Railway Museum at Perris, California.

***Below:* The motorman of this L.A.-bound Glendora train waits for two bells before departing Oneonta Park. The 300s were preferred to the 400s on both the Glendora and Santa Ana lines because of their greater speed.**

Ex-Northwestern Pacific 306 glides to a stop at Abila, just south of Watts, on the Long Beach line.

Former Interurban Electric Railway car 450 poses for the camera at Eighth and Alameda Street yard in Los Angeles.

The other segment of four-track line was on the Southern District. It extended south from 9th and Hooper Streets in almost a straight line to Watts. *Above:* A San Pedro train plunges through the smog at Amoco Junction. *Below:* This view from Slauson Avenue, looking due north, shows the Los Angeles City Hall on dead center of the right-of-way. The car in the foreground was the only former Pacific Electric passenger car to be repainted in Metropolitan Transit Authority's two-toned green and white livery.

Above: **Northbound 306 pauses on the Santa Ana River bridge. The Santa Ana line was almost totally rural. Today (1983) this location is adjacent to vast urban commercial complexes and one of the busiest freeways in Orange County.**

Below: **Los Angeles-bound 5088 departs Oneonta Park. The abandonment of the Pasadena Short Line and the Monrovia - Glendora were just days away when this 1951 photograph was made. The 5050 suburban cars simply couldn't maintain the rapid schedules of the Elevens that they replaced.**

FREIGHT OPERATIONS

When it came to hauling freight, PE was definitely in the big leagues. At its zenith, Pacific Electric was third among all carriers in origination of freight within California. Of course this was in conjunction with and as an extension of Southern Pacific, and that can lead to all forms of semantic arguments.

The services offered could be broken down into two categories. The first was transporting carload lots with citrus, building materials and oil field-related goods topping the list of commodities. The other category of freight was LCL, less-than-carload. Here PE had a fleet of express cars transporting parcels and mail for both Railway Express Agency and the Post Office.

PE's fleet of equipment was incredibly diverse. There was little or no standardization which made for a fascinating collection of motors and express cars.

Where did this diversity come from? Some pieces PE acquired in the Great Merger of 1911. Others were bought new. Still others were built in the company shops. A lot of equipment was acquired from other companies, primarily Southern Pacific subsidiaries as they were closed down. The old ethic of "waste not, want not" was company policy. And they did a magnificent job of extracting the maximum value from every dollar of capital invested.

Pacific Electric remained a quasi-independent freight operator long after the passenger operations had fallen to the ax. On August 13, 1965, it was finally merged into the Southern Pacific.

Today the freight business is but a shell of what it once was. The packing houses that supplied so much citrus and the oil that was frantically pumped from the ground are for the most part gone. Railway Express and its dogma of management inflexibility have perished in the bankruptcy courts. And the Postal Service is busily subsidizing other forms of transport.

***Below:* 1599 switches refrigerator cars in the Eighth and Alameda Street yard. This machine was constructed in 1923 by the company shops using the motors and electrical equipment from Henry Huntington's private car "Alabama." 1599, along with identical sister 1600, were fixtures in this yard for most of their service lives; a condition that posed a real challenge to the photographer attempting to get pictures of them. Security around this facility was always tight because of the extreme safety hazards and the constant threat of pilferage from freight cars. It took a lot of imagination to either talk your way in or sneak in to get pictures of these elusive monsters.**

Baldwin-Westinghouse steeplecab 1617 was probably the closest thing to a standard PE locomotive. There were 34 steel locomotives of this type, 13 of which were homemade in the Torrance shops. Up until World War II, these freight motors were painted red with yellow-gold lettering. Thereafter a more mundane black with orange stripes was applied to conform with the new diesels then being acquired by parent Southern Pacific. The photo was taken on the Santa Monica Air Line just east of La Cienega Boulevard.

1593 came to Pacific Electric from the Red River Lumber Company. When built in 1927, it was almost identical to 1617, but after an altercation with a lumber truck this motor was rebuilt with the unique box cab. This motor was one of the very few to survive the demise of PE. It, along with sisters 1592 and 1599, found its way to Buenos Aires, Argentina.

One of two gas electric-powered cars that were acquired secondhand from another SP subsidiary, Northwestern Pacific, and used as locomotives on the nonelectrified "islands" at San Fernando and Orange, 1649 can be seen on San Pedro Street deadheading to Torrance Shops.

In 1920, PE built this little switcher for shuttling cars about the massive Torrance shop complex. In latter years this tiny locomotive received an engine, hood and radiator from Los Angeles Motor Coach Company double-deck bus 1011.
Photo by the late Robert Loewing

Southern Pacific Steam Engine 1113 and a pair of freight motors switch the nonelectrified sidings near Wilmington on the San Pedro line.

Last of the *Golden Gates.* Sixty-year-old express car 1401 was days away from the scrapper's torch in this 1947 view taken at Macy Street Yard. Built as a passenger car in 1887 for San Francisco's Golden Gate Park and Ocean Railway, it migrated south in 1902.

Railway Post Office car 1407 departs the mail room at Main Street Station for the 57-mile run to San Bernardino. Pacific Electric was the last company to operate a trolley RPO in the country.

Railway Express Agency operations were centered in this terminal on the Aliso Street side of Union Station. From here, box motors were dispatched to REA offices located throughout Southern California and always adjacent to some segment of the PE system.

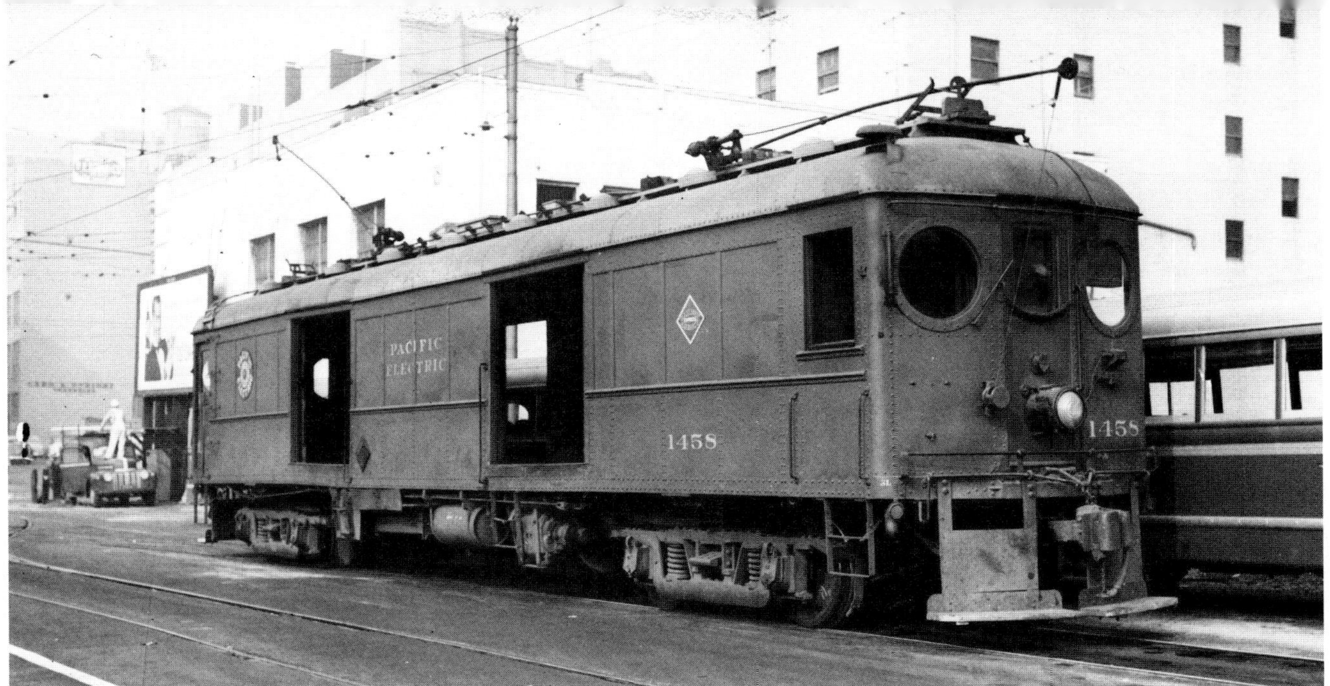

Top: Box Motor 1458 was a former passenger car from Southern Pacific's red electric lines around Portland, Oregon. In 1929 it arrived from Oregon and was placed in dead storage. Too good to scrap, PE rebuilt it into an express car. This picture was taken in the Seventh Street Yard adjacent to Main Street Station.

Left: 1452 rests among the weeds as it is loaded with mail at Whittier. This car was built by the old PE shops at Seventh and Alameda in 1915.

Bottom: 1465 was one of two "blimp" express cars acquired from SP's East Bay lines when they were closed down. She is seen at Macy Street Yard.

Former 800 series passenger cars, 1495-99, were the only examples of their car type to survive the great modernization of 1939-41. The Eights weighed up to 37 tons and certain cars were capable of speeds in the 80-mph range. Numerically, the Eights were the largest single class of interurban cars on the PE system. Though similar in exterior appearance, the Eights possessed a baffling variety of electrical components. *Above:* 1498 leads a string that includes three of these cars at Macy Street Yard. *Below:* A very early view of a train of Eights taken at Santa Monica.

Photo from Jeffrey J. Moreau

MOUNT LOWE—"THE GREAT RAILWAY TO THE SKY"

To contemplate what Southern California might have been like before the massive urban sprawl is like wondering what the world was like before the Egyptians or even television. Any conversation on the subject generally concludes that there was no world before the Egyptians or television!

Southern California was a far different and wonderful place back those many years ago. The sky was electric blue, the air clear and mountain fresh. The landscape was a serene and majestic desert.

From 1893 to 1937, the world enjoyed a Southern California scenic wonder more magical, more inspiring and, yes, at times more hair-raising than the best commercial attractions of the late 20th century. What scenic wonder? The Great Mount Lowe Railway! This was an enterprise created in the mind of David J. Macpherson, promoted by Professor Thaddeus S.C. Lowe, built with pick and shovel by hundreds of laborers and carried up those mountains on the backs of mules.

The whole idea was born in a series of proposals for first a toll road, then a railway from Pasadena to Mount Wilson. Several different schemes were proposed by various promoters, all of whom shared a common problem: lack of funds.

Thaddeus S.C. Lowe's name was committed to our history books long before the advent of the railway bearing his name. Prior to the Civil War, he was famous for his gas balloon exploits and with a particularly large balloon called the *Great Western* in which he contemplated crossing the Atlantic. Eat your heart out, Jules Verne! Of course, some of his efforts were beyond the technical capability of the day. Case in point was when he tried to fill *Great Western*—the New York City gas supply couldn't be delivered fast enough to cover the leakage from the balloon.

The Civil War was to bring him even greater fame in his efforts on behalf of the Union with his balloon *Intrepid*. He joined the Union effort at the personal request of President Lincoln. During the war, he made over 3,000 ascents, many over hostile forces, to gather intelligence about Confederate operations. This was no small feat, when it is considered that these balloons were lethal devices filled with highly flammable hydrogen gas. One stray ball of hot lead and instant Hindenburg syndrome!

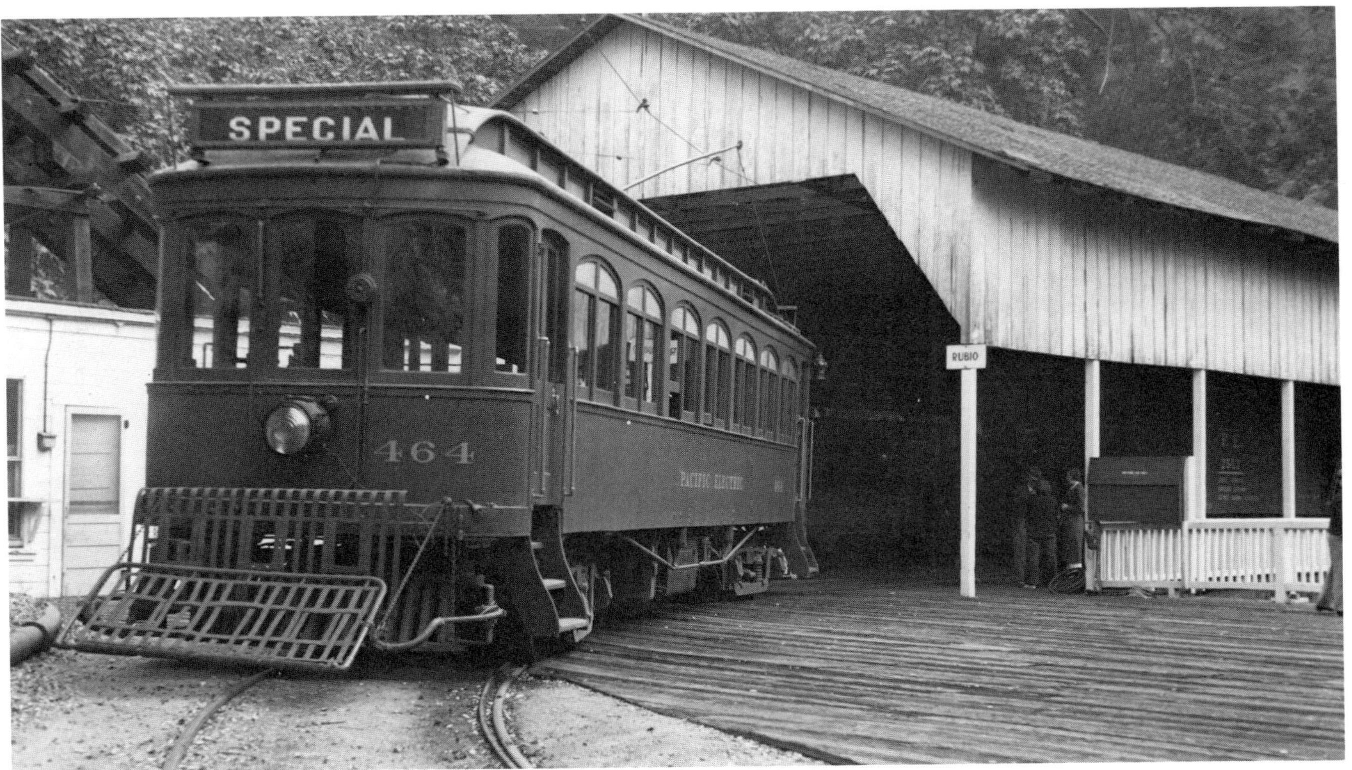

Car 464 poses for the camera deep in Rubio Canyon at the base of the incline. The trainshed was built to replace the Rubio Canyon Hotel which was destroyed by a landslide. The base of the incline railway can be seen on the left upper corner.
Photograph by Ernest M. Leo

Professor Lowe's astronomical observatory at Echo Mountain. When built in 1894, it contained a 16-inch telescope, a scientific marvel for the day. A windstorm destroyed this structure in 1928.
Photograph from the Collection of the late Martin O'Malley

Lowe invented a method of extracting hydrogen from water which freed his balloon from the dependency on city gas works for his lifting force. His service to the Union resulted in the establishment of the Army Aeronautic Corps and it was his observations about air conditions and inversion layers that resulted in the creation of the United States Weather Service. He was the first to take photographs from balloons. The battle of Fair Oaks in Virginia was probably won with information provided by Lowe's observations. A film titled *Up with Lowe,* detailing his Civil War exploits, was made during the 1970s by Walt Disney Productions.

In 1863, Lowe returned to Pennsylvania where he worked with gas manufacturing and developed a series of inventions, among them a method of creating ice with ammonia condensation. At age 55 in 1887, Professor Lowe, having made and lost several fortunes, decided to retire. In that year he moved to Pasadena, then the most populous city in Southern California.

Upon his arrival in Southern California he did what every "normal" retired person does, immediately becoming involved with gas manufacture (Pacific Lowe Gas and Electric Company); with ice (Citizens Ice Company); and with banking (Citizens Bank and Columbia Savings). And it was now that he met David J. Macpherson.

Macpherson had a plan for a railway up to Mount Wilson but couldn't get the financial support he needed. When Professor Lowe heard and saw this plan he immediately became enthusiastic. From this point the Mount Wilson railway was on in earnest.

Macpherson immediately set about surveying the route for such an endeavor. Two problems cropped up which were to change the plan and the ultimate destination of the railway. It was discovered that the decomposed granite of the hillsides up Mount Wilson was too unstable to support the railway without prohibitively high annual maintenance costs. To compound the problem even further, Lowe and company were unable to reach any sort of agreement with the owners of the properties atop the peak.

At this point, it was decided to change the ultimate course of the line and build up Echo Mountain.

The first stage of the line was a narrow-gauge electric railway from Mountain Junction on Lake Avenue, between Mendocino and Calaveras Streets in Altadena, to Rubio Canyon, a distance of about two miles. Here a small hotel was constructed.

The second stage was a funicular railway 3,000 feet in length rising from the 2,000-foot elevation at Rubio Canyon to 3,200 feet above sea level atop Echo Mountain. The gradients of the incline ranged from 48 to 62 percent. Two resort hotels, Echo Mountain House and The Chalet, were constructed on top of the mountain. In keeping with Professor Lowe's interest in the sky, a celestial observatory was constructed nearby. Every structure on the mountain was painted a stark white which gave the eerie look of another world. The line was opened to the public on July 4, 1893.

The funicular railway, or Great Incline, was an engineering wonder of its time. Conceived and designed by Macpherson, it took eight months to grade by hand. A chasm near the top was bridged by a trestle, named for Macpherson, which was 200 feet long and 114 feet higher on one end than the other!

In 1896, high construction costs along with interest costs exceeding 10 percent forced Lowe to default on his bond payments. The bondholders foreclosed. The line then passed into the hands of one Valentine Peyton who reincorporated the line as the Pasadena and Mount Lowe Railway. In 1902, Henry Huntington acquired the line for his Pacific Electric.

The cable-winding equipment for the incline was designed by Andrew Halliday's California Wire Rope

Company of San Francisco. (Halliday was inventor of San Francisco's famed cable cars.) The incline worked on the principle of counterbalance. Two cars were interconnected by a cable through a powered wheel at the top of the hill. As one car ascended from the bottom, its weight was offset by the weight of the car descending from the top. The cable used to propel the cars formed a continuous loop with a sheave wheel at the bottom of the hill. This system permitted the rapid removal and substitution of either car. There were three cars available: Echo, Rubio and Alpine.

A secondary cable was set parallel to the power cable. This one was stationary and acted as a safety device. A clutch or grip was attached to the underframe of each car. This grip was designed to lock onto the secondary cable should the car ever become detached from the power cable.

The track gauge on the incline was the same as the railway from Altadena and the Alpine division, three and one-half feet. An Alpine division car or its component truck could be hauled up or down the incline by substituting it for an incline car. Lowe hauled his four single-truck cars this way in 1896. PE added three new double-truck cars to replace Lowe's in 1906. At least two of Lowe's cars were removed from the mountain several years later. A fourth double-truck passenger car was taken up in 1912 and a motorized flat car went up in 1914. There was no other way to move cars on and off the mountain.

A 100-hp electric motor was used to turn the incline

Below: A glass plate negative, taken in 1893, shows one of Professor Lowe's "opera box" cars on the Macpherson trestle near the summit of the Great Incline. The Echo Mountain Chalet can be seen on the left. The trestle, named for David J. Macpherson, was an engineering marvel for its day. Although only 200 feet long, it was 114 feet higher on one end than the other. Today, the ride up that incline might be compared to riding a glass elevator up the face of a 200-story building without benefit of glass! *C.B. Waite photograph from Raymond E. Younghans*

Left: **The station atop Echo Mountain looked like this in 1910. The distant structure (center left) on the hill was Professor Lowe's observatory. The cable-winding machinery for the incline was located in the base of this structure. The great searchlight atop the parapet could be seen 50 miles away at night.**

cable. Initially, 300 storage batteries were used to provide electricity which in turn was generated by water power. A combination of California's arid climate and a suit over water rights soon ended that idea. Next a couple of gasoline engines were installed to generate electricity. This wasn't the most reliable method but it worked. After Pacific Electric took over, all power was furnished from the Altadena substation.

The final stage of the line, the Alpine division, was constructed from Echo Mountain to Alpine Tavern 5,000 feet above sea level and at the base of Oak Mountain (soon renamed Mount Lowe). This 6,100-foot mountain is located across Eaton Canyon from Mount Wilson. By line of sight, Alpine Tavern was a scant two miles from Echo Mountain, but because of the mountain terrain, three and a half miles of line were needed. There were 127 curves; the longest straight section being but 225 feet in length. Eighteen trestles were built. One of them, Circular or "Rim of the World," featured a 145-degree curve on a 75-foot radius at four and a half percent grade! This trestle afforded a spectacular view of Southern California including Santa Catalina Island, over 50 miles away.

One disaster after another plagued the mountain railway. Fire destroyed the Echo Mountain House on February 5, 1900. On December 9, 1905, another fire precipitated by a monster windstorm destroyed every building on Echo Mountain with the exception of the observatory. On February 12, 1909, a lightning strike high on Echo Mountain generated a landslide which destroyed the Rubio Canyon Hotel; one life was lost. A small transfer shed was built to replace the hotel. Another windstorm blew the observatory to the ground in 1928. Wind, rain and landslides played havoc with the upper line taking down bridges, power lines and tracks. It was as if the mountain were trying to drive off the intrusions of man.

The Depression of the 1930s reduced patronage to a point well below any profitability. A succession of events occurred which then sealed the fate of Professor Lowe's railway. On October 25, 1935, fire destroyed the Macpherson trestle on the incline. It was rebuilt with some delay. Then the worst that could happen did. Fire destroyed the Alpine Tavern on September 15, 1936. This left the tourist railway with no overnight facilities. PE applied to the California Railroad Commission for permission to abandon all service north of Mariposa and Lake Avenue in Altadena. The slow-moving bureaucrats in Sacramento had barely rendered a decision when nature rendered one of her own. On February 28, 1938, a massive cloudburst left the Alpine division completely useless. The only facility left was the incline. As a *coup de grace* vandals burned the incline powerhouse at Echo Mountain in 1940.

Today, little remains of the former line. The ravages of man and nature have obliterated the few remaining traces of the line. The upper division right-of-way has been graded into a fire road. In the late fifties and early sixties, the remains of Alpine Tavern and the Echo Mountain powerhouse were dynamited into rubble, an inglorious finale for what was once the greatest tourist attraction in California.

Here are two views of the Circular, or "Rim of the World," trestle with a spectacular panorama of the Los Angeles basin in the background. Echo Mountain can be seen directly to the left of the car in the upper photo; behind are Altadena and Pasadena. The lower picture shows Montrose and La Canada in the background.

Both photos by Charles Lawrence from the collection of Raymond E. Younghans

HORSESHOE
CURVE
ELECTRIC
31

FROM ECHO MOUNTAIN TO MOUNT LOWE

Opposite page, top: Looking both uphill and downhill in the same direction on the line from Circular Bridge. In later years car 31 was closed in on the mountain side and open on the other. This arrangement afforded some protection to the passengers from rock slides that plagued this line.

Opposite page, bottom: Car 31 in the bright morning sun at Horseshoe Curve. *Both photographs by Ernest M. Leo*

Right: Granite Gate near the top of the line. The entire Mount Lowe Railway was one engineering achievement after another. This one proved to be the straw that broke the camel's back. The costs of blasting and picking through this stone notch bankrupted Lowe's company.
Photograph from the collection of the late Martin O'Malley

Below: Alpine Tavern, at the top end of the line, offered hiking, horseback riding or just a chance to get away from it all in the pine-sweet mountain air. *Photograph by Charles Lawrence*

FINALE

Partially consumed by the scrapper's torch, these relics of another age are lost in time never to pass our way again.